Have Wings Will Fly

Compiled by Karen Coward of the Knowle West Domestic Abuse Project

We dedicate this book to all the survivors we have worked with, it's been an honour and a privilege to walk alongside you.

Published 2009 by Tangent Books
Unit 5.16, Bristol BS4 3EH

0117 972 0645
www.tangentbooks.co.uk

richard@tangentbooks.co.uk

Publisher: Richard Jones
richard@tangentbooks.co.uk

Stories compiled by Karen Coward of the Knowle West Domestic Abuse Project

Photography: Nikki Little http://nikkilittle.blogspot.com

The T-shirts in the photos were made by survivors for the Clothesline Project (South Bristol). This was originally an idea from America that was brought to Bristol by Community at Heart in Barton Hill. They ran the Clothesline Project for a couple of years until its funding ran out. We are able to continue its work by showing the display at raising awareness events, and running workshops for survivors to make and donate T-shirts (more information about the clothesline project can be found towards the end of the book).

Design: Dave Oakley dave@arnosdesign.co.uk

I would like to say thankyou to the funders of the project - Safer Bristol, and a special thankyou to the directors of the Knowle West Health Association for their ongoing support.

I would also like to thank my colleagues for their help in compiling this book and Nikki Little who donated her time and expertise to create the amazing photographs throughout this book. I would like to say a special thank you to the 12 people who very bravely and with heart and honesty shared their stories with us – THANK YOU.
Karen Coward

Contents

What is domestic abuse?

Domestic abuse is the misuse of physical, emotional, sexual or financial control by one person over another who is or has been in a relationship. This includes family members. Domestic abuse can include being threatened with abuse. Domestic abuse is usually by men against women, but not exclusively. Domestic abuse happens in all groups and sections of society. Race, sexuality, disability, age, religion, culture, class or mental health may have an additional impact on the way domestic abuse is experienced, dealt with and responded to.

Bristol Domestic Abuse Forum's definition.

Foreword

Domestic violence is the ultimate betrayal of trust in a relationship. It can break-up families, cause enormous suffering and is responsible for scores of deaths in the UK every year. Hidden away behind closed doors, domestic violence is much more prevalent than people might think, with around a third of women abused by a partner at some time in their lives. Victims can be rich or poor, young or old, white or black. What they have in common is the devastating impact domestic violence can have on them, and their families.

But there is some hope. Projects like the Knowle West Domestic Abuse Project are making a real difference. Their free, confidential services provide a life-line for many women in South Bristol. There is never an excuse for domestic violence, and victims should be provided with as much support as possible when they display the courage to speak out. This book provides fantastic examples of people rebuilding their lives after domestic violence, and will, I am sure, be an inspiration to many people who are suffering abuse now, or who have done in the past.

Dawn Primarolo

Labour MP for Bristol South

Introduction

The Knowle West Domestic Abuse Project (part of Knowle West Health Association) has the privilege of working alongside many survivors of Domestic Abuse and felt that it would be an encouragement to record some of the journeys of survivors who had moved through a difficult abusive relationship to a fresh start. We spent several months appealing for stories from survivors. We received responses from people from many different backgrounds who had heard of our appeal for stories via our website, through word of mouth and due to the publicity we had sent to other organisations. We received some great and varied responses and we hope the 12 stories in this book will both touch you and inspire you.

This book of survivors' stories is first and foremost for survivors, although we hope that workers who come into contact with those affected by domestic abuse will also find it insightful. In our experience when we are in an abusive relationship it often feels like a big confusing mess, where the person we love and who is supposed to love us, instead frightens and hurts us emotionally, mentally and sometimes physically.

This book will hopefully inspire survivors (and others) wherever they are on their own individual journey, to let them know that they are not alone out there, they are not to blame, and they have nothing to feel guilty or ashamed about. Although the journey to freedom can feel like a long and sometimes impossible one, it can be made. The following stories are from survivors – women & men – who have not only survived the abuse they endured as children or adults, but have gone on to thrive.

We also hope they will encourage you to find your own wings, and eventually learn how to fly!

The Knowle West Domestic Abuse Project

The Knowle West Health Association (KWHA) was set up over 20 years ago to protect, preserve and promote good health in the Knowle West area of Bristol; it is now one of the longest running voluntary agencies on the estate. It is managed by a Board of elected voluntary local residents, who are responsible for several projects under the KWHA umbrella.

Over the years the volunteers at KWHA were approached by local victims of domestic abuse looking for both emotional and practical support in the area and as awareness of KWHA grew so did the number of victims coming forward. Our volunteers built up strong links with other statutory and voluntary organisations on the estate and it was through these links that they were encouraged to look for funding to run a domestic abuse project. With the employment of a development worker about 7 years ago we were able to look for funding to get the project up and running and the Knowle West Domestic Abuse Project came about finally in May 2004 when we took on our first caseworker. The project is currently funded with short term government regeneration funding, that funding pot is managed by Safer Bristol and at present we are funded until September 2009 after which our future is uncertain.

The Knowle West Domestic Abuse Project now has two full time caseworkers and a part time administrative assistant. The caseworkers are trained Independent Domestic Violence Advisors, they offer two types of service to people affected by domestic abuse in the area: the short term crisis response is designed to practically support people at highest risk of significant harm, and is focused on reducing that risk. Also provided is a longer term outreach service, this is open-ended and client-centred to offer emotional and practical support and information. This support is offered through one-to-one sessions, group chill and chat sessions, or the Freedom Programme (more information at the end of the book). We also run an informative and up to date website www.knowlewestdomesticabuse.co.uk, support young people at a local comprehensive School, are one of four agencies that provide independent support at Bristol's Specialist Domestic Violence Court (more information at the end of the book). We also run raising awareness campaigns for local workers and residents, training days, and volunteer opportunities.

In 2006 the Knowle West Domestic Abuse Project was shortlisted for the Emma Humphries award for the quality of work we do with survivors of domestic abuse.

Have Wings Will Fly ...

It was a few years ago that I heard an old African fable that has stuck with me throughout the time I have supported people affected by domestic abuse…

Long, long ago in a village on the edge of the African desert lived a farmer who travelled for miles tending to his herd. While out one day he discovered an egg fully formed that must have fallen from a ledge on a huge cliff rising up from the desert.

The tribesman wrapped the egg and carefully carried it back to the village where he placed it amongst the other eggs in the chicken pen. Much to the villager's amazement an eagle hatched from the egg, and set out to live amongst the chickens. On a few occasions in the subsequent years the tribes tried to get the eagle to fly off, but the eagle refused to fly and continued to live amongst the chickens.

One day a visitor came and saw the eagle pecking at the ground amongst the chickens and was appalled. He asked the farmer why the eagle was acting like a chicken and not taking to the skies where it belongs – the farmer told him the story of finding the egg, and the eagle's refusal to leave the chickens.

After much negotiation the visitor persuaded the farmer to sell him the eagle, and set out on the long journey through the desert back to the cliff from where the farmer found the egg. He climbed the cliff with the eagle carefully wrapped in his back pack. With sweat flowing from his brow and his breathing laboured he finally reached the top of the cliff, he stood and surveyed the beauty of the rising sun across the floor of the magnificent desert.

The visitor carefully unwrapped the eagle, and gently held him in his hands, with his heart beating, and his hands shaking he threw the eagle up into the sky over the cliff top. He held his breath as the eagle floundered, wings not fully open the eagle started to fall from the sky – ' you are not a chicken, you are an eagle, fly' whispered the visitor, willing the mighty bird to open his wings and take to the skies.

Suddenly the eagles long wings spread wide and he soared up into the air. The visitor fell to his knees in thanks as he watched the eagle circle over head. The magnificent bird flew past him a couple of times as if to say his thanks, and then took off across the desert. The visitor flung up his arms and cried Fly Eagle, Fly.

All of us have wings it's just that some of us haven't learned how to fly yet.

I hope the following stories will inspire you to find your wings and be everything that you can be.

Karen. X

Love Me, Love Me Not

My childhood was maybe not the best, but certainly not the worst. Mum tried her best bringing six children up on her own.

At times mum was poorly and had to go to hospital and us six children would have to be separated into foster care for the younger ones and children's homes for the older. Unfortunately, there was never spaces at 'normal' homes and on four occasions was placed into a home for naughty children called Vinny Green. Being separated for my brothers and sisters and mum was the worst bit.

I think of these times as very sad. I believe all these events that happened in my childhood must make me the person I am today. And the decisions and past choices I have made have some bearing on events in my life. But then my brothers and sisters went through the same as me, and each one of us has took different paths in life.

At the age of twenty one, living in London, I had a great job, a house in Bristol, and a flat in London. At least three holidays a year, life was great. One weekend whilst in Bristol, I met him. Good looking, strong, popular, and so funny. He made me feel absolutely wonderful.

The first week I met him I wanted to leave my job and flat in London so I didn't have to be away from him. I managed to last a month, then finally gave up everything in London to move permanently to Bristol. I am still mystified what happened to me to make such a huge decision like that so quickly. It was as if he'd put a spell on me and "I loved him" so much.

Within the first three weeks of being in Bristol, looking back now it was quite obvious the signs that our relationship was certainly not on an equal basis. He would make subtle comments on my weight, or how messy my hair looked. It made me very conscious of my weight.

We had been seeing each other for nearly six weeks and he hadn't worked in all that time saying he couldn't bear to be away from me. His drinking was heavy but I was oblivious to most things at the time. My confidence was very slowly but surely being knocked and knocked hard.

This was the beginning of the next 14 years of my life.

Most weekends consisted of me at home alone and him out with his friends. He would come home drunk. I would shout and scream: "Where have you been, why don't you want to take me out". He would just say: "Shut up you fat cow, piss off out of my face". I would keep on and on, prodding him, poking him, wanting some kind of response, good or bad. He would lash out and I would cry lots, hoping he would now feel bad about his behaviour and I craved for him to cuddle me, tell me that he loves me, but it usually ended with me curled in a ball, lying on the floor, wishing he loved and wanted me.

During the next two years it went from being bad to really bad. He wouldn't even cuddle me in bed, he never wanted sex with me, which was such a massive rejection. The more he didn't want me, the more I wanted him. Even writing this down, I feel like I'm writing about someone else. When you put things down on paper, it actually seems unbelievable, that this arrogant, pig-headed, bully could have so much control over another human being.

On one occasion he came home very drunk, he picked up and held our daughter over the stairs saying if I didn't shut up he would drop her. Why did I not get my child and run out of the door for good? The reason is because I believed that he didn't mean it, it was the drink that made him do things like that. How could he not love us?

Another time after another night out things got out of hand and he had a knife held against my throat and my five year old phoned the police and told them what her daddy was doing, within ten minutes knowing the history of my husband, the police came with plenty of support but it still took five police officers to restrain him. I start to feel sorry for him. Not my daughter, not for myself, but for my husband. When he was released the next day he was: 'So, so sorry'; 'It would never happen again'; and 'Maybe if you'd not started, it wouldn't have kicked off'. That was the usual I would hear after an incident. He would cuddle me, and he would cry and tell me how important our daughter and myself was to him. 'He would die without us'. It made me happy as I now had him telling all the things I want to hear.

There were so many similar incidents, but not once did I press charges. How could I do that to someone I loved.

One day the spell that had seemed to have been placed on me fourteen years previous had been broken. He had come home after disappearing for two days, collapsed on the floor, wet himself. I then realised that before he'd fallen into his drunken coma, he had placed his pissed on, cocaine wrap on the bathroom sink to dry out. My 18 month old son could have easily picked it up, but thank goodness didn't. I felt that did it for me.

It took nearly five years for him to accept that I would never take him back. Our relationship now is fine, because of our children.

I grit my teeth when he lets them down so often. I will even say to my son, "Dad couldn't make it as he had to work". I don't do it for his benefit, I do it for our son. As my theory on children and parents is that children copy their parents, so if I pretend that dad isn't a complete toss-pot, then hopefully my son won't turn out one.

Recently I was at a fundraiser, and my ex was there with his new girl-friend, she seems such a nice lady, within an hour of being there she was asking my daughter "Can you find your dad, tell him I'm leaving if he doesn't come now". Where have I heard that before. Unfortunately, 14 years previously when I began dating him.

To sum up everything. I have two beautiful children. There's so much I'd change looking back but that's not possible, so I use most experiences and make sure I do things very differently. I feel so free. I like my life so so much. A friend sent through a poem to me recently and I think this really does sum up things for me.

The woman came from a man's rib,
Not from his feet to be walked on,
Not from his head to be superior,
But from the side to be equal,
Under the arm to be protected
And next to the heart to be loved.

I Am My Boundary

I remember the first time so clearly, every feeling, every emotion and surprisingly little pain, just shock. I reluctantly got into the car, newly purchased Marlboro's in my hand. He was taking a chance driving to get me after the drinks he'd consumed, but it was 1am on a Tuesday morning, so he was taking the risk.

The walk out of the house had certainly calmed me down after the row. The drive round looking for me seemingly had done the same for him. Neither of us was prepared to apologise just yet, but we were at least calmer.

"Take off your glasses," he calmly said, as we were about to pull away from the side of the road.

I remember thinking what an odd request that was, I thought I might have tear stained mascara on my face that he had seen, and to be honest I was just confused.

Smack! Smack!

What just happened? He's just punched me hard, twice across the face. Smack! And again!

He drove off. I'd never been hit in my life, what a strange feeling, not pain exactly, just disbelief.

Suddenly I was angry. I was crying and shouting at him, this fury desperate to be released from inside me. He'd just hit me! How dare he hit me!

We drove home. All I wanted to do was run. We pulled into our car park space behind the house, I sat for a second and then the urge to run came over me. Before I had chance to move, he'd jumped out of the car, opened my door and pulled me out by my hair. I was screaming and crying, but no neighbours came to my aid. He dragged me onto the floor and started thumping and kicking me on the ground.

The next day he couldn't have been more apologetic, bruises of the previous evening evident on my face and body. Our housemates had noticed too, but said nothing. They'd been friends with him much longer than I had with them, and besides they were from the same cultural background

as him, something they all had in common compared to my middle class background.

It was only after that night that I realised the situation I was in. From that day on things got worse. It was like one day I just woke up and realised that for the past 5 months I'd had no control over my life what so ever. We got up together, bathed together, and ate breakfast together. If I had to go into town, we'd go together. If I had to go to one end of town, and he the other, we'd both walk to where I needed then walk to where he needed. My money came in and I immediately handed it over to him. If I needed to buy something, I would ask him for some of my money and depending on what it was for he may or may not give me the cash.

I didn't even notice any of this happening, it was an unconscious, gradual process of losing my independence and confidence and what was really scary about it all was it seemed almost natural. This is what being in a relationship means.

And then 6 months later, the final straw; the realisation of what I'd become, what, so I thought, I'd allowed myself to become.

"Get your foot off the bed!"

"My shoes are clean, leave me alone. I can put my feet where I want."

"I'm only going to tell you one more time, get your feet off the bed!"

"No!"

It was the noise I heard first, not the pain I felt. A quick flick of his wrist and a sound like a spade being driven into soft earth. The point of the knife was thrust into my leg. The deep wound started bleeding as the shock of what he'd just done hit me.

I knew I had to get out; I had to leave. But how? Where do I go? What do I do?

I went to the doctors and asked him to make a note of the wound and my allegation of how it had happened. The doctor suggested I see a counsellor, which he recommended. I agreed to go, I was desperate for advice and expertise. I went to the counsellor. The counsellor suggested I go to the police. The counsellor must know best, so I went to the police.

The police were lovely, really helpful and sympathetic. They asked me if I had anywhere to go, I knew I had some friends that would help in the short term. The police said they would arrest him for GBH the following day. They would call me when they were on their way round, to check that he was in and to give me warning.

I walked slowly home, shaking and scared, but feeling empowered for the first time in over a year. I knew so clearly then that the "love" I'd been feeling was merely fear and dependence. I had been made to feel so small and worthless that I thought I needed to have my life, my money and my mind controlled. I was so used to keeping situations calm, not rocking the boat, when all along I was empowering him to continue ruling me.

I knew in my heart that I wasn't worthless, useless and pathetic and more than that I knew that I didn't have to be grateful to him for being my boyfriend.

I'd been given an opportunity; no, that's not true, I'd created an opportunity. I'd had the guts to stand up for myself and ask for help. I'd admitted to myself what I'd known all along, he was weak and pathetic and attacking and controlling me to make himself feel better and because I was caring and good I wouldn't admit that what he was doing to me was outrageously wrong.

They say the first step is the hardest, they say the realisation and admitting the problem is the beginning and believe me it's true. But the first step is the hardest because it's at this point that you realise what lies ahead of you, the strength you will need and the fear it will cause. But believe me it is worth it.

I didn't want to rely solely on friends and family, I wanted to move on myself. I needed to prove that I could get a home, a job, and a life by myself. But without the support and love and reassurance of these people I would not have had the strength to resurrect myself. Finally, a year later I went to see a counsellor, I knew I needed to so that I could get things straight in my mind. After a number of sessions I felt a weight lifted from me shoulders, I was free from him and ready to move on.

From that day forth I have been nothing but determined. By the age of 29 I owned two properties and had my own business. I have travelled the world and finally met a man who is good, kind, trustworthy, supportive and loving. We now share a wonderful life together and I know I created this life using my determination and strength. It was a hard journey, but I ultimately appreciate things more because of it.

Wolf In Sheep's Clothing

Things were great between me and my boyfriend until we moved in together. We had only been dating for about three months but decided to live together in the city after finishing university. I knew he was an alcoholic but he hadn't had a drink for about a year and it didn't seem an issue in our lives.

Once we moved we were both isolated as we didn't know anyone in the city. I started a computer course and spent a few days a week doing the course in the city centre. At this time my boyfriend started drinking. I remember coming home from the course one day, walking into the lounge and seeing him drinking cans of lager. I was shocked as he had had a lot of problems stemming from his alcohol abuse culminating in him hearing voices and attempting suicide, and to see him drinking again meant that his mental health was in a bad state. I remember crying that night just out of fear for him and what this might lead to.

Nothing happened that night but gradually the drinking increased and was happening on a daily basis. He managed to get some temping work but could never hold a job down for longer than a few days as he would be too hungover to go to work. Eventually he signed on and stopped looking for work at all.

He would get very jealous when I went to my course. Upon returning home I would be cross-examined, who had I talked to, sat next to, been with, why was I late etc. He was paranoid and I would have hours of being questioned before he was happy that I had not been cheating on him.

Even when we went out together with some friends upon our return home I would be cross-examined again. He would pick up on a phrase I had used whilst talking to someone and would ask my why I used that phrase, what I meant by it, why was I putting him down… he would pick at the smallest things making me feel that I couldn't speak to anyone at all as I knew it would cause a massive argument and hours of trying to reassure him when we got home. I had to watch what I said in front of others and to his face, I had to justify my actions, how long I was out, who I spoke to, why I had called my mum, why I didn't have enough money to give him for drink, why I didn't want to go to the pub to watch him drink himself stupid. I found that I had to remain sober to make sure that I watched what I said so I could handle his paranoia.

It wasn't just the verbal side of things, he was aggressive, smashed up our flat, threatened, bullied and coerced me into doing what he wanted. The worst time was when he had drunk so much that I locked myself in the bathroom. When I ventured out I heard him talking to someone so I went to see who was there. It turned out that he was talking to himself and was saying how much he hated me, that I was a bitch, that I didn't deserve to live and that he was going to kill me. He was having a full blown conversation with someone that did not exist. I was so petrified I crept back to the bathroom and locked myself in and sat behind the door in the freezing cold all night.

The next day he would be completely unaware of what had happened the night before (or so he said). He would never apologise because he never admitted he had done anything wrong.

Reading back through this I now wonder why I didn't leave earlier. The reason was that I was stubborn, my parents didn't want me to go out with this person, they didn't want me living on benefits in a flat in the city and I didn't want to live at home with them any more, I wanted my independence and living with my boyfriend I thought would give me this. I didn't want to admit that they were right, that I had made a mistake and didn't want to return to the village that I came from.

After putting up with this behaviour for eight months I couldn't stand it any longer. What made me finally leave was that he tried to strangle my cat, I thought I could put up with anything that he did to me but once he hurt my cat that was it! I had just started my new job as an administrator in an insurance company and I thought now that I had the means to support myself I could ask him to leave.

It was agreed that he would meet me at lunchtime from work and I would give him money to get the train back to London. He never turned up. I remember walking home thinking that I was not sure what was going to happen when I got back to my flat or what state he would be in. True to form he was drunk and that night went out to steal whisky from a local supermarket to get even more drunk. I lay awake hoping he would drink himself to death or at least drink so much he would pass out and not hassle me.

After a few days of agreeing to meet me eventually he turned up and I walked him to the train station. I bought him the ticket, gave him six cans of lager and watched the train leave with him on it! I never saw him again. That was 12 years ago.

After he left I was so happy to be on my own. It was lovely to walk back home to my flat and know that I would be on my own, I could do what I wanted when I wanted, could go to bed and sleep and not worry about being woken up or hassled. I could go out with friends for a drink and not be scared of the consequences. I could have a drink and not have to remain sober just to deal with him.

It took me a few years to be able to trust a man again, to be confident enough in myself to ask for what I needed and completely be myself without worrying what their reaction would be. It was even longer before I could be near a man that smelt of beer or that was drunk and loud without shaking and having to leave the room. When I spoke to others about what had happened I would always feel panicky and start to shake but this gradually lessened as time went on.

I never regretted ending the relationship, not for one minute did I wish I had not kicked him out. Although I was only with him for a year that one year did a lot of damage, if I had been with him for much longer I might have lost my ability to be quite so strong. My work as a Domestic Abuse Worker has shown me how lucky I have been to be able to leave this relationship so early on. When women experience emotional, physical and mental abuse for years it can be very difficult to leave, especially when confidence has been eroded, and all power and control has been taken away. In my personal and professional experience I know that the emotional and mental abuse is the most difficult to overcome and can affect people the longest.

This experience inspired me to want to help others experiencing problems like me. I spent three years training to be a counsellor, worked voluntarily on a self-harm helpline and as a volunteer counsellor for a few years.

After qualifying as a counsellor I then realised that I wanted to have a more hands on approach where I felt that I was really making a difference. I looked into working in Domestic Abuse. I was lucky enough to get a job working in a community-based domestic violence project. My job as an Independent Domestic Violence Adviser means that I am able to support women practically and emotionally. I support them through the court process – criminal and civil courts, with the police, bobby van, solicitor's appointments, Children and Young Peoples Services, emergency refuge accommodation and housing problems, and also emotionally by helping to run a support group, the freedom programme and offering one-to-one support. I love my job as I feel that I am able to make a difference and help women to plan for their safety when in an abusive relationship as well as to leave.

I felt that my personal experience along with my counselling background would enable me to help vulnerable people that are trapped in a violent and abusive relationship. I don't regret experiencing domestic abuse as I feel that it has helped me to realise what I want to do, to use my experience to help others and enable them to see that even though it seems like an impossible thing to do, to leave an abusive man is to have a new life.

Early Hours

Early hours 2005

Early hours of the morning and I sit not really feeling anything, emotionless, detached.

Maisy my dog creeps shaking from behind the settee and I look around at the home which means so much to me. The broken door, fire, tables, phone, cream walls stained with red wine.

Feeling my face puffy and bruised I start to cry and worry about all sorts of things. How yet again am I going to explain my injuries at work? How am I going to cope?

It is always like this after one of his drunken rages, a mixture of loneliness and shame overwhelm me. For years family and friends have worried about my injuries and been exasperated by my excuses. How selfish of me to burden others when I have always had the option to leave.

I know I've had enough but feel too weary and drained to do anything about it. Outwardly appearing happy, always the joker, humour a flimsy barrier, I really feel worthless. The constant drip of criticism, how useless, lazy,fat, ugly I am has chipped away at my self confidence. I hate myself.

Early hours 2007

It is over two years since I wrote with such despair, this is my story.

I met ? over 18 years ago and was instantly attracted to him, he was funny, handsome. The relationship developed quickly and he moved in with me.

From the early days it was obvious life with him was not going to be easy, I ignored the warning signs, I loved him, a feisty character myself and thought with counseling things would change, it was a challenge.

Over the years it no longer became a challenge, it wore me down.

Jeckyll and Hyde I called him, displays of kindness followed by days of ignoring me, then insisting on talking and ranting all night. The systematic sleep depravation took its toll I was barely functioning.

I would leave him letters telling him how I felt as talking or confronting him about his behaviour was pointless. He refused to acknowledge anything was wrong, minimilising the situation or blaming me for provoking him.

Slowly I lost everything, my spark. I became a non person, my feelings needs irrelevant. He enjoyed pointing out my shortcomings, having always been extremely self critical, I hated myself.

I knew I had to go and it was not an easy decision to make. His family had always been a huge part of my life and the thought of never seeing them again was at one time incomprehensible.

The offer of a flat spurred me on and I made secret plans to leave. The ensuing weeks were a nightmare, terrified he would find out I became a nervous wreck.

I planned to leave whilst he was at work, but on returning home his car was still on the drive, he had decided to take the day off so hastily had to cancel the removal van. A visit to his family made the day even worse, I had not seen them for ages because I was aware I had to emotionally detach myself.

On returning home he turned nasty, the usual how ugly, useless, embarrassing I was. I asked him if I was so embarrassing why he was so keen I visit his children, he replied 'I wanted them to see the mess you have become' acutely aware of how ill I was looking. It was the final straw.

Over the years I had learnt to live with walking on eggshells and dealt with the havoc in an extremely passive way. You lose the ability to feel, it's as if you build a wall around yourself a coping mechanism, but that day I saw the look in his eyes, listened to his cruel words and became hysterical, leaving with virtually nothing but a few cuts and bruises.

That was seven months ago and I now live in a lovely flat, with huge support from family and friends rebuilding my life.

It has not been easy but I never thought it would be. Some days I wake up positive ready to take on the world, by evening a blubbering wreck dealing with emotions I hadn't allowed myself to feel for years. Any change in routine made me shake, but I am getting there.

I have never regretted my decision to leave, I am now relaxed and regaining my confidence, catching up with old friends and have holidays planned. Always believing myself to be stupid and weak I realise now I was really quite strong and smart I had to be to survive.

I have found writing this extremely difficult but if it only inspires one person and helps give them strength to leave an abusive relationship it will be worth it.

If I can do it anyone can!

Living The Dream

I was the youngest of three children. My dad was hardly ever there; he even volunteered to work Christmas Day! He controlled the family. I thought that no one could love me because I was overweight, curly hair, lazy eye (three operations before age 5 still couldn't correct it), frequently mistaken for a boy and had a stutter so avoided talking. People would say "You're not as pretty as your sister, don't suppose you're as clever either".

I wasn't allowed to talk to boys, even though I went to a mixed school, I was constantly bullied.

We had to do as we were told. Elders and people in authority were always right. My mum stood by and watched a doctor needlessly vaginally examine me at 14, when I next needed to go, she told me to 'do as the doctor said' so I didn't go.

At 15 I was allowed a boyfriend. I got pregnant and was taken for a termination, nothing more said. That termination has haunted me all my life.

At 16 I had slimmed down, had an op to straighten my eye and was controlling the speech. My father pushed me to leave home. I had just met a man aged 21 who was getting divorced and had a nine-month-old child. He seemed so grown up. He wanted me to move in with him, which I did as I felt I had no choice and of course he loved me! He didn't work, and didn't allow me to.

He quickly separated me from what few friends I had, then gave me the dream of a baby. I was pregnant by 17. He would disappear for days, supposedly seeing his other child (which he never did). He would drink for days, leaving me alone in the flat in a strange area with no money, no food, no TV. After the baby was born he was great for the first four months. Then we got a rented house closer to his family and got married (my parents were pushing me to marry, I didn't want to).

On our wedding night he told me that he could do whatever he liked and that's when the violence really started. He had previously just slapped me around. He was hardly ever at home, always at his dad's. But he still expected that at whatever time he walked in that I would have a cooked

And one day
I will reach
the top!
You left me
at the bottom!
FREE
FROM
your
THREATS

meal waiting for him. The agonising over when he would be in to have it was terrible because if the meal was left too long it would be no good and have to be cooked again. Sundays were the worst as he would be in bed sleeping off Saturday night's drink, get up and go the pub and expect a full Sunday roast when he came back, but even though the pubs shut at 2pm then, it could be anytime that he came home. So I couldn't do anything or go anywhere with the kids. I felt so alone.

My parents had moved 100 miles away and when I did see them dad just lectured me and then took my husband out drinking! My sister lived in Canada and my brother was a recluse. My husband's parents had seen me with black eyes etc and they said nothing to him. I wanted to leave and he said he'd get our child taken off me because I'd had a termination, and I believed him and stayed. Then he wanted another baby. I said I couldn't while it was like this. He was really attentive for six months, still drank, but not violent. As soon as I got the positive test he booked me for a termination and said he didn't want the baby. But I did.

During the pregnancy the violence got really bad. He started raping and anally raping me and watching porn and really beating me up and throwing me around by my hair. When the baby was 10 days old he punched me in the face whilst I was breastfeeding him. He kept me awake all night pestering for sex and then disappeared during the day. One day when I was dropping off the eldest child at playschool I tried to sneak in and out without anyone seeing my bruised face. When I picked her up, someone gave me a card for a solicitor and said 'they will believe you'. This was my turning point.

We separated for the first time when the baby was five months old, got back together, separated again and then finally separated when the 'baby' was two years old. The only support I had was from the solicitor who believed me. I didn't tell my parents much as they didn't think I should be single parent of two children and that I should work at my marriage. They didn't believe any of the violence, even after seeing boot marks all up my legs. So I never revealed the sexual side of the relationship.

It was difficult as my husband wanted to come back, but for the first time me and the kids felt happy. We could go out, I could eat!

He didn't want to know after a while, never saw the kids and never paid a penny for them. In total I was eight years with him.

I went and did voluntary work and worked as a mother's help (basically cleaning and babysitting), but it was a life! Every weekend me and the kids went roller skating, the park and swimming. I was very underweight through lack of food, but felt slim and attractive. I got a babysitter for when the kids were asleep and went to aerobics, studied for a GCSE in Psychology and Mathematics and started dating! I joined a dating agency because back in the 80s it was hard to meet someone when you had kids. Did I have a great time! I went out with men from all sorts of backgrounds, even dated a couple of millionaires! The funny thing was, I got marriage proposals on a weekly basis and bouquets of flowers on a 2-3 times a week basis. I could not believe that I had once felt so bad about myself. My father was NOT impressed! He said that I should behave as a 'mother of two does'. Then after three years I met a man who didn't try to prove himself to me. He 'ticked all the boxes'- yes I had a check- list as I wasn't going to make that mistake again!

We got married and I had a third child (I call her my bonus child). My husband encouraged me to register for childminding and provided the financial support. He had a good job and encouraged me to do things. My dad of course hated all this as he had lost his control over me and the kids.

We moved to the west country by the sea when my third child was three years old (my second husband's dream) and the house was full of children every day. I loved childminding as did my own children. I earned good money and could buy what I wanted.

My husband taught me to drive (and this opened up the world to me). But I still felt a horrible sadness inside and I went for counseling. This really helped as through hypnotherapy I discovered that I had built a brick wall around me and I was inside with my first two children, the youngest still a baby. Through counselling I knocked down the brick wall and after that nothing stopped me. I attended many training courses for childminding and received national recognition for my childminding work and officially became the best childminder in the country in 2006.

I took up running, swimming and went to discos. I worked voluntarily supporting victims of crime, especially domestic abuse, achieved a teaching certificate, got diplomas in childcare, psychology, studied for an NVQ in Childcare and Education and a Foundation Degree in Early

Years. At one stage I was working full time, teaching two nights and attending university one late evening (plus the discos, concerts etc!) All this with my husband's support. When the going got tough, he encouraged me. He taught me all the IT that I needed to know to get me through the courses. We have days/nights out together and great holidays. We have had difficult times (but not related to our relationship) and we have supported each other and talked our problems through

I childminded for 15 years until our youngest was almost 16. Then I got a management job for a national charity working with women who experience domestic abuse.

I am living the dream. I am proof that you can succeed no matter what life throws at you.

I Am Alive

I am female, 35 years old and a survivor of domestic abuse. I use the word survivor very loosely. It has been ten years since my divorce and I am still feeling the after-effects. Some days I feel far from being a survivor. Some days I feel so disconnected with the world I don't know how I am going to survive the next five minutes, let alone the rest of my life.

I had one perfect year of marriage. Then I had a year of wondering what the hell had gone wrong. Then, for the rest of my marriage I wanted out, but couldn't – or more accurately wouldn't make the final leap into the unknown.

Towards the end of the marriage it was far from pleasant. He had systematically separated me from all my friends and would fly into a rage if I contacted my family. He made me feel insecure, doubtful, terrified and alone. All I wanted to do was to make him happy, yet all I seemed able to do was to anger him over the smallest little thing.

All this was before he started seeing other women. When this started – things got worse.

I was never what you would call a confident person. I am nowhere near having the looks of a supermodel, I was always a little bit chubby, of average intelligence – but I was a wife. I was loved. I think it took so long to leave him because I didn't want to admit to my family or to myself that my marriage had failed. That I had failed.

When I look back at what had happened, I can barely believe I survived. It got to the point that I didn't care what he did to me or how he made me hate myself. He could belittle me, control me, install fear in me, abuse me and reduce me to a quivering wreck. All that mattered to me was not admitting to anyone that I was in trouble, that I needed help, that my marriage had failed.

Many things happened during these terribly bleak years. I allowed things to happen to me that I am not proud of. One thing that I am truly ashamed of was my attempted suicide. After another argument about his other women, he left the house. I just wanted it all to end. I didn't want my life to end; I just wanted some peace, some space, and some clarity.

I Am FREE
TO SPREAD
MY WINGS
GRAB HOLD WITH BOTH HANDS TO LIFE!
HE CANT HURT YOU NOW

I swallowed some sleeping tablets and lay on the sofa. I still remember all this time later how calm I felt. The inner peace was amazing. I knew that very soon I would be asleep and all my problems would vanish. It honestly never crossed my mind that I may never wake up, that I may die. I'm a little confused about what happened next. The way I remember is was that he came back and found me. He called my parents and then he called an ambulance. Surely this cannot be true. Surely he would have called an ambulance first. Surely he wouldn't have called my parents first to gloat over the fact that I may be dead?

After I was released from the hospital, I had a revelation. "What the hell am I doing?" Even though I had had this amazing breakthrough, I still could not leave him. Life went on.

When I finally left him, I realised how supportive my family was. I had never really been that close to my brother's wife – but she proved several times over how I could count on her and rely on her as a friend. I no longer class her as a sister-in-law. She is my sister. I also became extremely close to my mother. We always used to be a close and loving family before my marriage and after the marriage ended we became even closer. It sounds corny but I recall the saying "a mother and daughter's bond is the strongest and also the hardest to break".

I truly believe, even with the support of my family I wouldn't have got through this without the friendship of one particular person. I had gone to the home of one of his work colleagues to try and track him down when he went missing for a few days on a drinking binge. The wife of his work mate (whom I had never met before) had no idea what to do with me when she opened her front door and I burst into tears. She told me she didn't know how to advise me, so she took me to her next door neighbour (who was divorced).

The first thing my new found friend did was hug me. Even before she was told who I was or why I was there. She hugged me. Wow! I then spent several hours sat on her sofa, crying, drinking coffee and being hugged. Over the following weeks, months, years (and to this day) I am supported by my friend. She never judges me, never questions my actions, never told me what I should do and never made me feel inferior. Looking back, I must have spent thousands of hours with her over the following couple of years. I used to turn up at the crack of dawn and in the middle of the night, always to a hug and a smile. This was the first time, in a long time, that I felt safe. I felt secure. It was an incredible feeling – knowing I could be myself, say or do what I wanted and have no fear of being beaten because of it. She's been, and still is my guardian angel.

I remember clearly one thing she said to me all those years ago "if I could cut the next five years out of your life I would". At the time I didn't fully understand what she meant by that statement. Now I do understand. Those first 4-5 years after the divorce were horrible. I cannot explain the range of emotions I had (or am still having). One morning I would be fine, I'd wake up and feel great – really optimistic but by the afternoon I could barely string two words together, stop crying or stop myself being terrified that he would turn up at any minute and drag me back into the nightmare I had finally escaped.

So many things happened that led to me leaving him. I will mention only two. The first was when he moved one of his girlfriends into our home whilst I was still living there, and the second was when he came to my mother and father's home with this woman and assaulted my parents.

After this woman moved into our home, my parents begged me to spend one night with them – to get some peace. I went home the following morning to walk our dogs. I assumed he would still be out on one of his drinking binges – but he was there and so was this woman. All hell broke loose. Fists flew and blood was spilt. That day, my mum, dad and my brother's wife came to get me and take me back to live with my parents. That day, me, my dogs and my cat moved out. That, I thought was my new beginning. As we drove home I remember being horrified that people knew I had failed my marriage. But I also had a small patch of hope. It was the hope that things would now get better. That afternoon, my parents had a telephone call from him. It was threatening and abusive. Mum informed the police. Later that night he arrived at my parent's home with this woman in tow.

Chaos reigned between them banging on the door, the neighbours calling the police and the police arriving. When the police arrived en-masse, he was banging my father's head against the side of the wall and the woman was attacking mum. The police subdued and took him away. She was also taken away (she didn't want to be left on the street alone in case she was attacked!). How the hell were we going to attack her? Dad had a stroke 3 months before, Mum had a heart operation a couple of months before and had both just been beaten to a pulp. That left me! A quivering wreck – unable to comprehend how much my life had spiralled out of control. Out of control so much that it was my fault my own parents were being attacked.

This happened on a Sunday night. Three days later I was sat in a solicitor's office filing for a divorce. Ironically, the day I filed for a divorce was my three year wedding anniversary. By seeing the violence I was so used to being used on me – now being directed at my parents, I had finally realised how low I had allowed myself to get.

That was the turning point. I didn't see the pure, white, shining light at the end of the very long tunnel of abuse. All I saw was a tiny little glimmer of light. That glimmer was all I needed to keep going. To survive. To live.

I am still dealing with the after effects of my marriage and divorce. All these years later and I am still dealing with certain issues, certain doubts.

I still have a tremendous fear of abuse, of being pressured into doing anything I don't want to. This has had an effect on all my relationships since. I am either very controlling or end the relationship before it even has a chance to really start. I sometimes find my self having panic attacks if someone is standing in a doorway blocking my exit. I would know this person quite well, and be in a familiar place – but for some reason I sometimes find the need to flee if a door is blocked. I still find it incredibly hard to walk into a public place I am not familiar with. I find it impossible to socialise with people I do not feel extremely at ease with.

I also have an issue with anger. This I find really strange – I have never classed myself as an angry person. On bad days, I find I really have to struggle with my self control so I do not lash out at people, either physically or verbally.

The past year has been easier. I have changed my career path and now work with a local charity that does amazing work with disadvantaged students. My work colleagues and my managers are extremely supportive and understanding.

What I do not want is for you to finish reading this and feel sad about what has happened, and about what is still happening to me. I am more confident and for the majority of the time I really enjoy my life. I can do what I want, when I want and not be fearful of what will happen to me. I will not be beaten and belittled anymore. I will not feel scared.

I still flash back to when my friend said she wanted to cut out the next five years of my life. At the time I prayed that she could and would do this. Now, looking back I am glad she couldn't. Those horrid, bleak, awful years defined who I am today. Those years made me the strong, confident (sometimes bewildered and unhappy) person I am now.

The light at the end of the long tunnel started out as a tiny glimmer. Today, and most days the light is very strong and bright. Every day that light shines brighter for me – I feel good to be alive. I am alive.

I am alive.

FREEDOM
ALCOHOLIC
FEAR
HURT

I Am FREE
TO SPREAD
MY WINGS
HURT You Now

THERE'S LIGHT AT THE END OF MY BLACK TUNNEL
I AM MOVING TO MY NEW HOUSE
THIS WILL A BRIGHT NEW START FOR ME AND MY CHILDREN

Hit ME,
Hit ME NOT
Hit ME

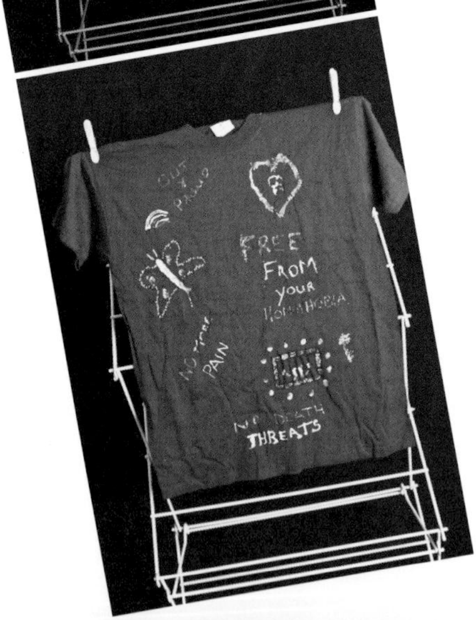
FREE FROM YOUR
PAIN
THREATS

When you found me I was...
happy
friendly
ambitious
outgoing
intelligent
confident
hopeful
loving
You have made me...
confused
bruised
scared
lonely
doubtful
embarrassed
closed
I will find myself again without you

Taking Control

When I met him I was feeling very vulnerable. My son's father had let me down badly and I was now a single mum trying to work and bring up my baby on my own. Although my son was now four years old and I had a good job as a Legal Secretary and my own flat I felt something was missing and I was very lonely.

He made me feel really special. At the end of our first date he kissed me on the cheek and told me he would always look after me and that I would never have to worry about anything ever again.

As the weeks passed he would phone me all the time, turn up outside of my work to walk me home and arrange impromptu nights out. At the time I was flattered that I seemed to mean so much to him and he wanted to be around me all the time.

My family were concerned they felt he was taking up too much of my time. I would continually break arrangements I had made with them because he had arranged for us to go somewhere else. I was particularly close to my sister but recently had been spending less and less time with her. Eventually I explained to him that I could not cancel on her again and I would have to go out with her. He was upset that I did not want to spend the time with him but said we could do something the next day. It was not long after this night out that he told me my sister had made a pass at him. Relationships between me and my family members became very strained and when I announced our wedding they refused to attend.

Before our wedding I was due to undergo major surgery and so he moved into my flat with me and my son so that he could look after my son while I was in hospital. As I lay recovering in hospital I began to realise that this man was not the Knight in Shining Armour I had once perceived him to be. There was a very dark and sinister side to his character and I had apparently been the only person oblivious to this.

My family were only allowed to visit when he was at work and he refused to bring my son in to visit me. This was particularly difficult for both me and my son as we had never been apart before.

When I returned home I was still confined to bed. He would leave for work taking my son to the nursery. He would leave my medication and pain killers with a glass of water beside my bed. I would struggle to get to the toilet and longed to have my mum beside me, helping me and comforting me but this was not allowed.

Before my scarring had time to heal I discovered I was pregnant. Now I felt really trapped! He picked on my every word, telling me constantly that I was not good enough, I couldn't speak properly, I was a bad mother to my son, I was stupid, fat, ugly, no-one else would want me because I was a mess. His favourite song he would sing to me was "if I were a rich man I'd get treatment for my Psycho Wife". I constantly felt insignificant and worthless. I felt isolated as I could not tell anyone what was happening, I had messed up again!

During my pregnancy I lost so much weight they threatened to keep me in hospital. I couldn't allow this to happen because I could not leave my son alone with him again. I hoped that once the baby was born things would improve but I was wrong.

Every time I left the house I was timed, if I was not home at the appointed hour he would tap on his watch and ask where I had been. The look on his face was enough to put the fear of god into me. I knew then that was it and he would go off on one. When we were out I would need to watch what I said or I would be questioned when we returned home. He had seen the way I looked at him! How I had flirted! That I was having an affair with my sister's husband! The accusations were never ending so I began to isolate myself further for fear of doing the wrong thing and having to pay the price.

I remember on one particular occasion I had been to visit my brother, as the time went on I became more and more apprehensive. I was constantly looking at the clock and trying to think of excuses to leave. My sister-in-law told me not to be so stupid that I was with my brother and he would understand this but I knew different. When leaving their house I ran through the many excuses I could give for being late and eventually decided to tell him that I had ran over a cat and because he knew this would upset me and that I would have to stop and see what could be done, I would be late home.

I didn't like the person I had become I would lie and be underhand in order to see people. I would pack my swimming costume and towel say I was going swimming and make sure it was put straight into the washing machine on my return so he wouldn't know I had visited my sister. It all sounds so bizarre now but that was my life.

For thirteen years both me and my son suffered at the hands of this man but thanks to my daughter bringing me to my senses I managed to escape. I knew deep down that I would have to leave but did not have the strength to do it. When my daughter asked me if her husband would treat her the same way that "Daddy treats you" I knew I had to go.

I contacted the Housing Association and told them about the abuse me and my son had suffered. They put me on the priority list for re-housing and within three months offered me what was to become my new home. I remember receiving the call to meet the housing officer. I was anxious that someone may see me but excited that things were moving. The house was a mess; dirty in need of refurbishment, but it was my ticket to freedom. As the tears rolled down my face the Housing Officer told me not to look at the house as it was but to look at the potential. I assured her that these were tears of joy.

For two months I had to sneak around, decorating and preparing my new home so that I could move me and my children. Once it was habitable I arranged to move the kids' beds and our clothes while he was at work. I was so scared that he would find out before we could go but it all went according to plan. When he called me that night to ask what was going on it was the best feeling in the world to tell him I had left and had my own house.

It took me a long time to recover. I remember being surprised at how depressed I was at the beginning. For the first year I had to attend counselling and was prescribed anti-depressants. I no longer knew who I was and it took time to re-discover myself.

Eight years on there have been many ups and downs along the way but I can now think for myself. It took me a long time before I allowed myself to get close to someone again but two years ago now I moved in with my partner and we recently bought our first home together.

Just over a year ago I saw a job advertised for a Domestic Abuse Admin Worker and I was lucky to have been given the job. I have just been accepted on a counselling course and upon completion hope to be able to continue working with the Project as a Domestic Abuse Response Worker.

What Is A Survivor?

What is a survivor? My mum was a survivor.

More than 60 years ago my mum married my father. It was wartime (WW2) and many people rushed into marriage not knowing what the future held for them or if they would ever see an end to war and live a normal life again. Both my parents were in the army for the duration of the war.

When the war was over they set up home in Bristol. My mother was not from Bristol and found it was difficult (now with a baby) to become a wife and mother in a strange place. Mum had only ever lived in a small village. She had no family here and struggled to please a very domineering husband.

During the next couple of years they had purchased an old terraced house with no electricity. We used candles for lighting and I remember being stuck on the stairs in complete darkness when a candle blew out. The house was very damp and freezing cold in winter. The toilet was down the garden with a door that had huge gaps at the bottom where the wind blew icy cold.

My parents had five children and things were not going well. My mum's sister asked if she could stay and get a job in Bristol as there was no work in the village. My mum eagerly looked forward to having the company of her sister. However, this proved to be the beginning of the end of the marriage. My aunt became pregnant whilst not married. This was frowned upon in those days so mum took over the upbringing of her child. By this time mum was completely domineered by both her husband and sister. Her sister had two more babies, but it was mum who had to take these two to the adoption agency. There was no chance that she could manage these two in addition to her own 5 and her nephew.

It was around this time that mum could no longer carry on with the way things were. It also became clear to her that my father had been responsible for these three babies. Close to a nervous breakdown she sought help and threw them both out of the home. They came back later and took their son with no warning. Mum had raised him as one of her own and to her it was like having one of her children taken and was never again allowed to see him.

Eventually the house was repossessed, paying the mortgage was impossible. We eventually were given a house in Knowle West. A palace.

Mum had a huge struggle raising us. She had coped with violence, emotional abuse and fear. Then she had to cope with hunger (no social security then), worry, breakdowns and the guilt of her family not having what most other kids had.

That worry and fear was never shown to us once my father had left the home. From then on mum made sure we had lots of love, praise, support for whatever we wanted to do. All five of us left school with jobs to go to. We never felt deprived, it was always our house where we were allowed to play with friends. We had boundaries and set bed times. A very happy family life.

Yet things could have been so different. We don't have bad memories of childhood. Although we remember some of the bad times – they are overshadowed by the good times.

Mum's determination not to be a victim, made her a survivor. It didn't happen overnight but it taught me to keep fighting for what is right.

Mr Angry

I do not recall Mr Angry entering my life but I remember being shocked when I was told that he was not my 'real' dad. I remember Mr Angry as an angry man who seemed to enjoy beating my mother and hurting me. His influence on my life was negative in the extreme and it caused me to have a terrible fear of men. His actions are beyond my understanding and his drunken frustrations with his own past should never have been worked out on my mother or me.

I can recall many times of isolation, fear and loneliness when I think about this period of my life. I remember, quite vividly, one occasion when I was alone late in the evening and in the dark, no older than four or five. I was feeling terrified, alone and confused. It was a traumatic experience for a little boy to feel so utterly abandoned. I can remember I was wearing short grey coloured trousers and white underpants. I had soiled myself and I had excrement running down my legs and into my sandals. I was smelly and needed an adult to help me but I could not find one. I remember having the fear of what Mr Angry would do to me if he found out. His heavy slaps and pokes were something I often endured when no one was looking, and the fear of his anger was a terrible burden. Unless something like this has happened to you, it is difficult to convey just how traumatic an incident like this can be to a small child, and how many scars remain in adulthood. Just recalling this time in my life can stir up deep, overpowering emotions within me, causing me to be uncontrollably upset, even as I write.

I once got a severe beating from Mr Angry after one of his dogs had choked on a piece of pipe from the shed and Mr Angry held me responsible because he said I left the shed door open. He dragged me around the house, shouting, pushing, shoving, and shaking me. His spit used to hit my face when he did this and I was always terrified. This is another memory that brings a wave of emotion when I recall it. It was after an attack like this one that I developed a facial twitch and stopped communicating with people. My mother took me to a child psychologist and he sent me to a 'special' class in another school once a week. It was at that class that I made a papier mache mask of an angry face. I kept that mask until I was fifteen. No one ever realised that the mask was Mr Angry, the cause of my silence and my twitch.

I have too many memories of arguments and beatings. On one occasion I can remember him poking me in the chest so hard that I had small finger-sized bruises all over my chest for weeks afterwards. On another occasion, I had messed up his tools in the garage and I was dragged upstairs by him and he held my head under cold running water before throwing me on my bed and locking me in the room. I recall whimpering alone in that room, and unable to catch my breath.

On another occasion Mr Angry literally hung me upside down by my feet out of the back bedroom window. I was terrified of being dropped on the concrete flags below in the garden. I remember the feeling of hot urine running over my stomach as he held on to my ankles. He was shouting and lowering me up and down, as if he was going to drop me. The pebble-dashed wall cut my knees and elbows as I screamed and apologised to him. He had caught me lowering my action-man out of the window on a piece of string. It was just a game. The fear of this incident left me with a terrible anxiety in later life that would manifest itself whenever I was up ladders, or on the edge of a sea cliff. I also had a fear of dogs that I took with me into adult life.

Mr Angry used to make me stand in the kitchen if I was naughty. The dogs were kept in the kitchen and they used to growl at me. He would shout 'guard' and they would sit and stare at me. If I moved, they would growl. This was a horrible thing to do to a child. I was traumatised by the fear of being eaten by dogs. Later, as an adult, I lived with such a fear of dogs that I would break into a sweat and shake, even at the sight of a small dog. I always tried to hide my fear because I was so embarrassed.

The abuse I had suffered at the hands of my stepfather was extreme. I was regularly hit, shouted at, and poked in the chest until I was bruised. Watching him argue and strike my mother was also a regular occurrence and I often hid under my bed and cried late at night when I heard things being smashed and my mother screaming.

The most haunting memory that I have is of him hitting me with a belt after stripping me naked and then destroying my bedroom in a rage. I was five or six when he first did this to me. I do not know what I had done to deserve such a brutal punishment and he attacked me as if I was a grown man. Firstly he ripped out all the furniture in my bedroom, literally pulling them out of their fixings. He smashed them with his feet and fists as he hurled them down the stairs. He pulled down the curtains in his rage and even pulled up the carpet until there was just a hill of mess and broken wood. He then turned on me and pushed and pulled me and ripped my clothes. He stripped me naked and then hit me with his belt.

I do not know where my mother was when this happened, I just remember cowering in the corner and crying and shaking for a long time afterwards. He also once sat on my little chest and force-fed me with sprouts because I would not eat them. I remember the feeling of choking on vomit when he did this and thought I was going to die. He must have weighed at least fifteen stone. He was a fat man with a moustache and I was a skinny kid with a pale complexion.

Today, 32 years on, I am happily married with seven wonderful children. I have put the past behind me and moved on with my life. I now work with vulnerable people and my personal experience helps me to understand their needs. I wrote and published my own autobiography and the process was very liberating. I will always be a survivor of abuse but the abuse no longer occupies my daily life. Despite Mr Angry, I am happy and loved. He remains lonely and burdened with his guilt.

A Chance To Be Myself – Evie's Story

My name is Evie. I was abused by a family friend when I was 13 and by the time I met my partner I was still rather shy and withdrawn. I met Rob when I was 19 and he was 33. He seemed so wise, so very understanding. For the first time I had found someone who I could really open up to and it was great. I moved in with Rob about six months after meeting him and at first everything was oh so good (ring any bells?).

He would be so loving, and I was feeling so good for the first time in years. As for sex, well he had made that become everything that I didn't know existed. Thinking back now I realise that even then he was starting to control my life. He was picking out my clothes, getting my hair done etc he even got me working. And slowly but surely contact with my own family, my mum and my sister was becoming less frequent. There was always some excuse you know, when I would say that I was going to visit he always came up with some excuse not to "Oh Evie, I thought we'd have a nice day out" you know always something. I just didn't see it sneaking up on me, couldn't read it.

It all changed about six months later, he came home one day and told me that his four kids (that I did know about) were coming to stay for a while. "I'll understand Evie if you don't want to do it but I have to, they are my kids and their mum is a drunk and they could be taken into care". I stood by him, who wouldn't? Poor wee souls, I can still remember the first time I saw them, four wee souls, lost, confused and everything they owned in carrier bags, coming to stay with a dad they hardly knew and me! Becky aged 9, Sonia and Sally (twins) aged 8 and wee Davy aged 7.

Those kids accepted me from day one and to this day I still feel so privileged that they did. I most probably didn't give them as much as they needed and I feel bad about that. I tried, that is all I can say.

Not long after they moved in everything started to change. Rob started gambling and he was becoming very agitated and angry at the least little thing. The first time he hit me was when a phone bill had came. I was

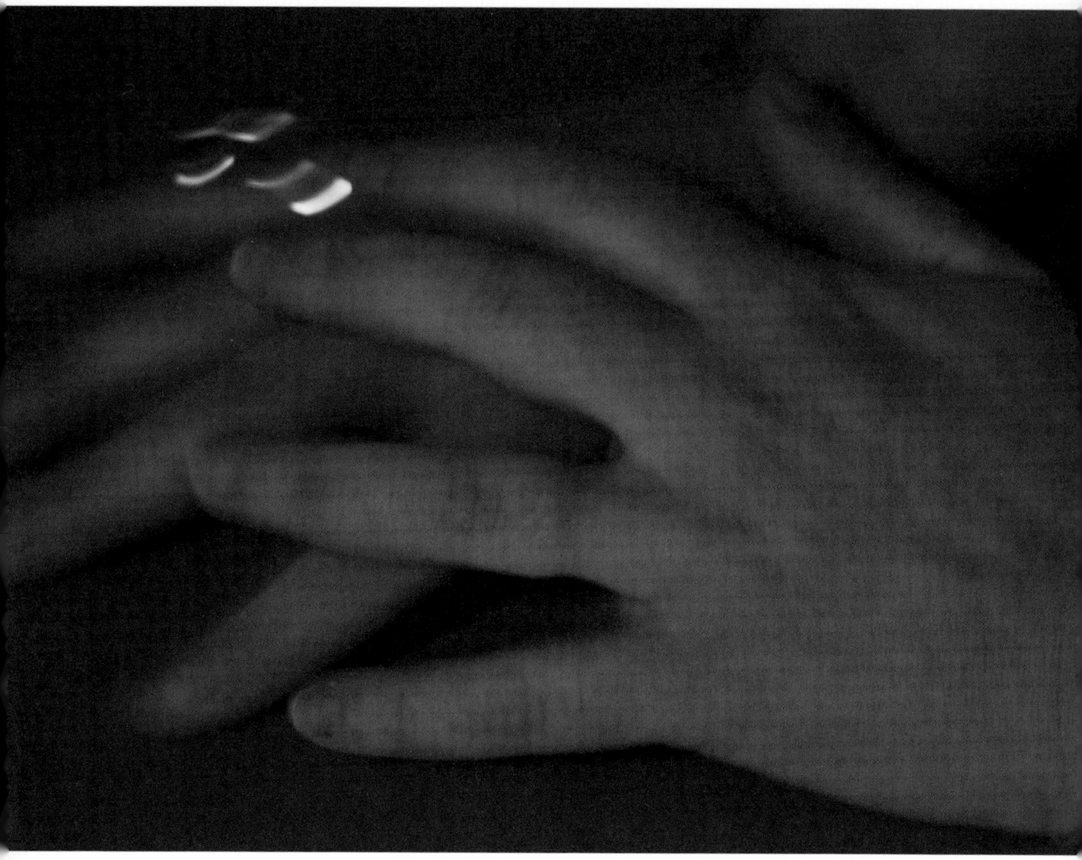

making dinner in the kitchen and the kids were up stairs when he came charging in waving the bill in front of my face…

"What the f**k is this? Who the hell have you been phoning?"

"My mum, she's been upset and I was just trying to comfort her" (my mum was in an abusive relationship you see and I was, well, just trying to be there, I didn't see her hardly at all but I still phoned now and again).

"Well it will just have to f**king stop OK, we can't afford bills like this!"

"We could if you weren't gambling so much:"

BANG!

I never even saw it coming, just felt my head snap back and my cheek starting to burn. To say that I was shocked is an understatement and at first I didn't even react just stood there looking at him.

"Oh Evie I'm so sorry, I didn't mean it."

He came over hugging me telling me that I was right and that he shouldn't have done it. I couldn't say or do anything, I was so conscious of the kids being upstairs and I had grown up with it you see, so I just turned around and got on with making dinner and by the time the kids were in bed I had forgiven him.

This went on for about a year, sometimes a slap, sometimes a kick, always "so sorry" and me always so forgiving. But I was becoming cowed, you know what I mean? That eroding of your character, the tiredness, the acceptance! But all of this was nothing compared to what was to come (oh how I wish I had run then, but I still loved him and the kids you know). The kids' mum was starting to get better and we had decided to let her have them for the weekend, they really missed their mum and they needed her. I was happy for them and they were happy, that's what mattered.

"Let's have a night out Evie, you deserve it, a nice meal maybe".

Things had been really good for a while and I was hoping we were starting to turn the corner. Rob had been trying really hard to try and control his temper, even going to the doctor to get help. So out we went…

The night started with a nice meal and then on to a pub and we were having a great time, really enjoying each other's company, really talking for the first time in ages. The subject of sex came up the way it does between couples and we started talking about fantasies and did we have any. He told me that he had fantasies about watching me having sex with someone else because he knew what they were getting (me being so good), I told him that I had fantasies about being with a stranger, not that I would but that it felt exciting thinking about it (a sitting duck!).

We then went on to talk about other stuff and I had forgotten about it really until we left the pub, we were both pretty drunk and I was staggering a little and as we started walking towards the city centre to get a taxi.

"How about it Evie, fancy trying it?"

"Trying what?" I said.

"Going with a stranger and I'll watch, it will be so cool just to live out our fantasy huh".

At first I was "Don't be daft" and eventually after lots of convincing and loving words from him it became

"Anyway how are we going to do that", as I said sitting duck!

"Just stand on the corner there and wait for some guy, you pick and if he asks if your looking for business say yes, take him up the lane and give him a blow job, I don't mean full sex or anything and I'll follow behind and watch".

And so it was I found myself standing on a street corner thinking what on earth are you doing but feeling excited as well I must confess. Reality soon changed that feeling I can assure you. The guy I picked was just an ordinary guy, seemed pleasant enough.

"Looking for business love?"

"Eh yeah," I said.

"How much for a blow?"

"Eh twenty quid."

"OK," he said.

And so I took the guy down the lane and as soon as we were in the corner he started to grope me and pushing me down to my knees. I think maybe I went into shock. I was aware of what he was doing but I believe my brain just went into automatic shut down you know. He zipped himself up and walked away, just like that. I was still on my knees when I heard the footsteps turned around to see Rob walking towards me with the most loving happy smile I had seen for ages.

"Oh Evie, thank you that was so cool, what a turn on, you ok Evie?

Oh Evie please say that you enjoyed it to, I'd feel so lousy if you didn't enjoy it".

I stood up and I can still think of the thought processes even now. How much I had hated it, how dirty I felt, how much he had enjoyed it and it was only once right, why make him feel bad, just go with it.

"No I'm fine Rob, it was just different to how I had imagined it that's all, but it's fine, it was cool".

When we got home and Rob started kissing me and telling me how wonderful I was. I thought, 'it's going to be ok!' How very wrong I was. He started asking me to describe what I had done. Suddenly he punched me in the face and I fell backwards onto the floor.

"Did I tell you to let him do that Evie, did I? F**king cow! F**king loved it that much did you?"

BANG! Another punch, splitting my lip.

BANG! A kick this time, into my side as I lay there.

I got one hell of a beating that night, kicked, punched, slapped, even a cigarette stubbed out on my back, and during it all his voice: "F**king cow! Me thinking you hadn't liked it, feeling guilty and all the time you had loved it, you bitch".

I awoke the next morning to the sound of him breaking his heart. I lay there feeling like I had been hit with a ten ton truck. Every part of my body was sore. I didn't know what to do, my mind was a complete blank, numb! He noticed I was awake and immediately came over put his head on my breast and started the usual.

"Oh Evie what have I done, god I'm so sorry…" Sobbing and crying. "Oh god the kids, I've messed up everything, what am I going to do? Please forgive me, I'll go get help, I'll do anything".

It's amazing the strength of love you know. I loved Rob with all my heart and soul, and this hadn't changed that. The love was still there, it's like your brain getting split in two. One half can't believe that the monster last night was this man, my Rob and the other half knows this is so, but you love and that sways the outcome, tips the scales. I put my hand on the back of his head and stroked his hair. "Shush Rob, it'll be okay, we can do this but you have got to get help okay, real help."

"Yes Evie I will, I will, thank you, thank you".

There wasn't even time to talk properly, the kids were due back soon.

I Am FREE
TO
SPREAD
MY
WINGS
HURT You Now

38 YEARS/NO MORE
• PEACE & Quiet

Hit ME,
Hit ME NOt
Hit ME

You made Me fLY.
Thank you
It was your problem
Not mine.

When you found me
I was... happy
friendly
outgoing
intelligent
ambitious
hopeful
loving
You have made me...
confused
bruised
lonely
closed
embarrassed
without you

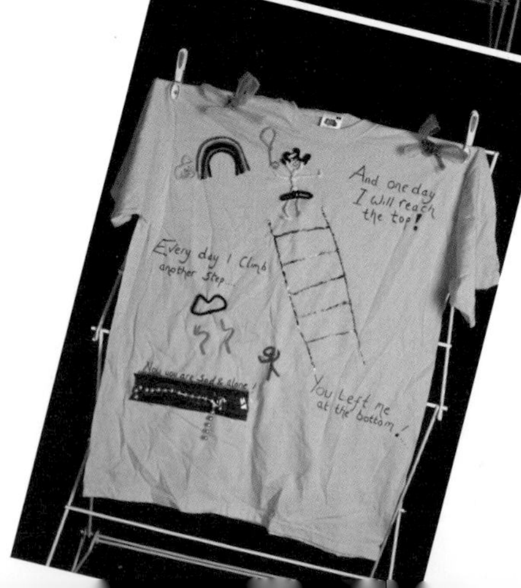
And one day
I will reach
the top!
Every day I climb
another step...
You left me
at the bottom!

Up I got, showered, checked myself in the mirror. I stood there looking, hardly a mark once I had put on my clothes. Underneath a mass of bruises. There they were "Evie, that's the kids back". I took one last look, slapped a smile on my face and went down to greet the kids. I would like to think that the kids weren't aware of what went on in our house and to this day I have never spoken to them about it. I only know that I tried my best to make sure that they never got to see or hear anything. That mattered to me.

Rob was so guilt ridden for weeks, months. He treated me with such kid gloves, apologetic, loving. I had even started to have some contact with my family again and Rob even encouraged it. He went for help (or so I thought, I found out later that he never did) and for the next few months we set about repairing our relationship. The kids were still visiting their mum every weekend but I wouldn't go out with Rob, couldn't bring myself to. But after about eight months of this constant attitude I decided that I would try a night out. Big mistake! Again we went for a lovely meal, then on to the pub and even onto the dancing. It had been a great success. It all started again when we left to go get a taxi.

"How about trying it again Evie?"

"What?" and I felt my stomach drop down to my shoes.

"C'mon Evie, it will be different this time, I know what went wrong."

"No Rob I don't think so".

"Oh great I've tried so hard for months, how much longer have I to feel guilty Evie huh! How many times can I say sorry?"

"I'm not asking you to feel guilty Rob, but it happened and I just want us to put it behind us that's all."

"I just want it to be right this time Evie, after all it was your fantasy too. I want us both to enjoy it just once, I can't even fantasize anymore because of what happened. C'mon it will replace the old memory if we can put it right".

"Oh f**king great, you don't even want to help do you, just want me to keep on feeling like shit about it don't you". Bang! Slapped me across the face. "F**king bitch, give me my keys." He grabbed my handbag and took my keys.

"Just go home to your f**king mum you bitch, go on go".

I looked at him and I could see the absolute madness in his eyes, I turned around and started walking away, I was going to mum's. Rob followed along behind me shouting abuse until he caught up swung me around and started laying into me.

"Where you going huh? Get back here and do as you're told".

I tried to get away but I couldn't and he continued to kick and punch me until I gave up and gave in. I had three different men that night and afterwards when Rob took me home I had to describe exactly what I had done until Rob managed to satisfy himself. I am ashamed to say that I was well and truly broken that night and I admit I still grieve for the person I was then.

I was a prostitute for nine years, four years on the streets and a further five years with clients coming to my house. You may wonder why I did not escape, and that for any abused partner is the million dollar question isn't it? Life had become this is the only way to describe it I suppose.

The kids stayed with us for six years until they finally went back to their mum. I know now why she had become what she became. He broke her too.

I could tell you many stories of the abuse I got both from Rob and my 'clients' (the beatings, the rapes) but that's another story I guess. I was a living zombie. I no longer saw my family, that stopped completely and I had no friends. Complete and utter isolation apart from the life I now lived.

I may have stayed there forever had it not been for the one other thing that changed my life. I had a daughter. My beautiful, wonderful, amazing little girl. I hadn't been on the pill you see for years and had thought that I couldn't have kids. I was always very careful with clients so I knew that Rob was the father. I can remember the phone call to tell me my test had been positive. I couldn't believe it. I told Rob and he was elated. We all moved to another house and everything seemed to change. I no longer did any of the 'bad stuff' and Rob appeared to have a complete change of personality. When Alice was born Rob became the perfect husband and father. He was like a different person, and for a while we were like your perfect 'happy family'.

Alice for me was just so perfect. I ate, drank and slept my wee girl. She was the light of my life and still is. In fact all the kids had been. My only reason for carrying on. When Alice was about one year old the other kids finally went back to stay full time with their mum. I was so very happy for them. Despite the love that we had for each other I knew that nothing could compare to their mum.

I know what you must be thinking, but believe it or not Rob had been a very good dad to his kids. It used to amaze me to watch him with them. But after they left it was like they never were. "Why don't we ask the kids round for dinner Rob, we haven't seen them since they left (six months ago).

"Why the hell should I? They haven't bothered with me have they".

And so it went. Rob started becoming very jealous of the relationship I had with my daughter, about how much time I was willing to give to her. The old Rob started to resurface, the agitation, the anger. I started to worry about where it was leading. The first time he hit me in front of Alice was when I decided to leave.

It took me two years to finally break free from Rob and it was the toughest thing I have ever done. But I did it.

That was four years ago now. I would like to say that I have my life completely back, but there are times when I get depressed. But I don't regret leaving, not for one second. My daughter is eight now and we have a wonderful loving relationship. Every day brings new wonders and I can see my daughter have the chance to be 'herself'. I hope she always will be.

I hope anybody out there who is still being abused will take the plunge. It won't be easy and sometimes you'll think you can't do it but I'm here to say you can. Everyone deserves the chance to be 'themselves' to find out what kind of person that can be.

Getting Away From A Terminator (The T) – A Survivor's Tale.

I gave the moniker 'Terminator' as my tormentor has not stopped at the time of writing, and continues to use any means to grasp at the final straws of controlling me.

It's difficult to know where to start, I was in a relationship that lasted for 22 years, until it was abruptly ended by police intervention. That's why I am alive to tell this tale.

T's own a sickness, which is unfortunately not recognised by most professionals, and almost impossible to prove in court.

The first time T hit me I was only 16. I left him and didn't see him again for 10 years. Then we met again and fell in "love"; actually it was obsession and control on his part, but he was charming. By the time the T hit me again we were married. The bruising was high on my thigh where no one would see it and it was extremely painful and lasted for 5 weeks.

Then along came our children, just 18 months apart in age, and when they were 3 and 5 we moved overseas. I had a very successful career and when I was working in the City, the T used to make snide comments and denigrate my work in front of others. He didn't work hard, preferring instead to drink hard and put in little effort as a professional. He was seen as "a nice bloke" who wouldn't hurt a fly, but underneath lay a seething hatred and anger. I never did find out why, and I no longer trouble myself with the question.

The T had trouble finding work abroad and trouble making friends. He was deemed as cold and odd and he didn't fit into the culture. He managed to get a couple of contracts, but generally spent the time drinking.

T resented my business success, as he realised I had broken the glass ceiling in a man's world.

Our maid looked after the children, and T had all the privileges that came with my work. He had affairs, he was abusive and started hitting the children as well as me after drunken weekend binges when he

disappeared for days on end. We used to cower in a bedroom hoping the T would not come after us, when our maid had her time off.

He forced us back to England using threats and bullying, but he was always charming in front of other people. We travelled back via Thailand and he had unprotected sex with a prostitute, using my money as he hadn't worked for four months. I started to drink very heavily. I was devastated by this disgusting behaviour. He took pleasure in telling me what he had done, and he had made a "mistake". But he didn't ever say sorry. We had the children with us. It was too late to go back by then, and the abuse really started in earnest.

In the UK he had an HIV test but wouldn't give me the results. He forced me to have sex so he could abuse me further. A refusal meant a punch or strangulation or a slap – as I quickly learned.

He cashed in our investments without me knowing, and lived on my savings while unemployed, the premise being it was "our" money. He took a job in Ireland and stopped coming home for weeks on end, using my credit card to book weekends away for two, and jewellery. I was drinking heavily to forget, wishing it would all go away and wondering how things had got to this.

I was pretending to everyone that everything was ok when it wasn't, and I was slowly falling apart, under his approving eye. He was supposed to send money home, but never sent enough, and he used to say "If you want to feed your f**king kids, then use your money." My savings slowly got eaten up. I never saw pay slips or a bank account where he would have been paid, so siphoning off money was a long-term goal. He had to leave the job as the children were distressed. He blamed me.

He was unemployed again and using my savings. He cashed in joint investments without my knowledge, and slowly asset stripped the marriage. I don't know where he put this money. It's gone.

When I told him I wanted a divorce, I was rewarded with four broken teeth, bodily and facial scarring and a fractured cheekbone. He said that if I told anyone, he would take my home and my children and make me stand up in court and be declared an unfit Mother, because I was an alcoholic. I didn't call the police. His mother saw my injuries, and so did other members of both sides of the family, but it was a dirty little secret, and no-one wanted to help.

He went to the dentist with me to ensure I told the dentist I had been mugged. The T told my father I had caused my own injuries and the T was believed. My Dad died believing this story.

The T started another job where he got a company car given to him. I was not given a choice in selecting it. He would not let me drive 'his' car. I had to take the bus or walk everywhere. His car was lovingly cleaned and polished while the home was left to rot and fall apart or appliances were suddenly 'broken'.

He isolated me from family and friends and made decisions about attending functions. He picked massive arguments just before a function to ensure I was too upset to attend. Without my knowledge he stopped my mother from coming to see me. He told people I was an alcoholic and was drinking 1.5 litres of vodka a day. My father's partner phoned around the family and spread this gossip on T's behalf. I eventually became dependent on alcohol to see me through my days.

The T had to attend courses in Europe. One time, he arrived home with 9 litres of vodka and handed it to me saying: "Hurry up and kill yourself, I hate your f**king guts". I was trapped.

The violence escalated. I had facial and body bruises on many occasions and wouldn't go out until they had disappeared. When he came home he ignored me, and refused to eat food I had cooked. The T bought lots of household cleaners. He wanted 'his' floors washed with thin bleach, and 'his' toilets cleaned with thick bleach. When I told him where to stick the bleach, he tried to force a bottle of it down my throat. I was regularly punched, slapped, strangled to passing-out point, knocked out cold twice, had my head split open, screamed at, threatened, sexually abused and financially deprived. I used to bury my face in a cushion hoping he wouldn't hit it again, and curl into a ball to protect my body. I wasn't allowed to have the things normal people have. The children – none of the family cared about them and what they saw. It was all okay.

Each time the T abused me, I never gave in. When I was drinking I still interacted with my professional associations and I won a very prestigious award for my work. T was livid, and I saw cold hatred in his face when I told him about it. This event was followed with the last time the T hit me. I was amazed I eventually got back up again. I realised that the next time he hit me I would be dead, and it had to stop. I called the police. They took him away and prosecuted successfully.

Nearly two years later, he has not been allowed back to the house. He has a criminal record. The T should have got a jail sentence, but he went to court a day early, pleaded guilty and walked away a free, rich man without giving me the chance to utter a single word. I completed a victim witness statement, to add weight to the severity of his offences. He charmed all the family on both sides to believe his behaviour was my fault and I lost my family. He has worked Family Alienation to perfection, and I am left without support except for my mother and two sisters-in-law. I am a pariah, because I told on the T.

What I haven't lost, is my life and my children, seeing them grow up, my sanity and happiness or my friends who have remained constant. Money… T's love money and lots of it.

Many people cannot comprehend how one person can inflict such appalling behaviour on another. The ones who understand these patterns of behaviour are those who have experienced it first hand.

While I was drinking and being abused, I used to write notes in a diary. I have dated photos of broken furniture, made notes of when he left broken glass in the freezer, when he left a chainsaw on the kitchen floor, blade upright with no safety catch. I made notes when he put furniture polish on the walking surfaces in the home to ensure someone (including his own mother) had an accident, and when he used to pour baby oil in the shower to make it slippery. There was no concern about injuring the children; his mission was to have me declared unfit or to cause me permanent injury or death, while giving me no choice of leaving him. I am under no illusions regarding the T's actions. Proving it is another matter though.

After he'd left, my house was broken into twice by family members, terrifying the children. When my father died; I was last to know about it; the T was present at the time of his untimely death.

The mind of a dangerous and abusive person deviates in ways that are difficult to explain or prove – especially in court. Most normal people would not think to do the kind of things a T is capable of doing. This T has never said sorry.

My children still want to see the T, but they may be open to further abuse and harm. I make notes of anything they say to me. I write it all down and maintain a detailed record.

This T is trying to get to me via the courts. He doesn't want to pay for his children. He has harmed them in many ways, including leaving them without heating and hot water for three months, and depriving them of gifts, and then using gifts to bribe. The T's mother enjoys inflicting this behaviour on them too.

The children received counselling, until he started litigation for more contact, so it has been put on hold. I carry a huge burden of guilt for allowing them to be exposed to the abuse for so long, and for not climbing out of my drinking hole sooner.

I will not take any more abuse. I will not allow my children to be abused. I am fighting back. I am in control and this particular species of T hates that. Part of his control was as an alcohol enabler. I am writing this to show that you are not alone, and you can walk away from a T, whether they are male or female; whatever your relationship, gender, or status.

When you take the first step you take control. You are in charge of your destiny. It's happier alone until you find new friends away from a T.

Don't take ownership of, or for a T; they don't own you either and it's not your fault they are like they are.

For me, after achieving sobriety, I realised I had lost my confidence. Some of that confidence returned, but there's no quick fix. Having a life free of fear and abuse is paramount.

When you say "enough!" you diminish a T's power and control. They can't cope with that loss and they flounder without their victim.

Finally, my tale hasn't quite finished, as this T still wants and wants and wants. I don't think he will ultimately succeed.

I stand strong, but outraged that we are still experiencing this abuse in the 21st Century. Nothing scares me now, except the realisation that you are reading this and maybe being abused.

"If it doesn't kill you, you can only get stronger." So plan, and take action. You CAN do it.

Step out the Victim's hidey-hole and into the Survivor's Sunlight, and embrace your power and take ownership; reach for it because it awaits you. Become a survivor.

Then, bring it on and stop being frightened. Face your fear head on - it isn't easy for me to say this as I have spent years living in fear. The bottom line and your ultimate goal is self-empowerment. That is your ultimate weapon against a Terminator. By the way, I'm not perfect.

Past the Horizon

I have been thinking about a story I heard as a child:

An elephant strode the sun-soaked plains. They spread before her as infinite and untamed as her own soul, filling her with the joy of being a creature alive in the beautiful world.

One day, she fell into a hidden snare. Before she understood what was happening, she was taken to a zoo and a heavy iron ring and chain were placed around her ankle and attached to a spike in the ground. At first she fought to break free with all her mighty strength and independent will, but the ring burned into her skin every time she struggled against it. Eventually, frightened of the pain, she stopped trying.

The zookeeper kept his prize adequately. She was fed and given water, but she was also forced to perform tricks that were unnatural to her, to entertain the crowds.

The elephant's life continued thus for many years. The zookeeper eventually removed the iron ring, knowing that she had become so accustomed to its grip that she would not notice its absence. It was true. Though the elephant cherished the distant memory of her freedom, she was resigned to the daily routine that she felt would be her lot until death parted her from the world.

One morning, a monkey was passing and noticed the elephant's tears.

'Why do you cry?' he asked.

'Because the plains still call to me, though it is an eternity since I felt the blessed grass beneath my feet and saw the land stretch to the horizon.'

'Then why do you stay here?'

The elephant explained about the iron ring and the agony when she pulled against it. The monkey smiled and pointed to her foot. The elephant looked down and was amazed to realise that the restraint was gone. She was free.

My monkey's name was John.

I met my husband, Stuart, 13 years ago. I had just arrived in the UK with all the fearlessness and pride of a woman just out of her teens and eagerly drinking in her first experience of independent life. He presented me

with a stable father figure. My love for him grew rapidly and usurped my desire for travel and adventure.

Abuse crept into our relationship with stealth – almost imperceptible at first - flares of temper, assertion of control, vindictive comments, wounding remarks about my appearance and personality. Then it began to turn physical. I actually can't remember the first time he grabbed me. The tricks of memory have moulded most of the incidents together. The sound of his heavy footsteps running up the stairs. The panic as I don't have time to reach the bathroom – the only room with a lock. The vision of his face, crimson, veins bulging.

Afterwards he would give in to my tears, calm down and rock me in his arms, as though he were the hero who had seen off the beast.

In my periphery, I glimpse his hand reaching towards my head. The gesture is meant in tenderness; he just wants to sweep away a strand of hair from my face. I flinch automatically, squeezing my eyes tightly and ducking my head – only for a moment, but he notices. 'Don't be silly. I'm not going to hurt you'. He laughs at my 'foolishness'. I am silent.

To the world outside our door, we were the ideal couple. I smiled and played the perfect wife. I could never mention the abuse to anyone. Friends and family would have listened and been supportive but the admission would have weakened and humiliated me. I wasn't even certain that it was abuse. He would grab, shake, push and drag me about, but he never punched me and bruises were rare. Perhaps we were merely walking that grey border between abuse and 'normal' marital argument. Stuart would always apologise afterwards and tell me how much he loved me. (I was later to discover that this pattern of behaviour – building up only to tear down - is common in cases of domestic abuse, which makes it difficult to break the cycle and leave.)

I had been raised in a strict Christian home to parents of the marriage-is-for-life generation. I had sworn before God to stay with Stuart until death and so accepted the path I had chosen as my lot – for better or worse. I knew that someday his rage might push him too far and my life would end…but I loved him and so I stayed. I convinced myself that love was about sacrifice.

The psychological erosion was just as dangerous. His comments would chip away at my self-esteem. I was 'stupid', 'ugly', 'clumsy', 'couldn't do anything right'. I came to believe that I deserved the poor treatment. Whereas in the beginning I had argued back, fragment by fragment my will was broken until eventually, I accepted it all in silence.

I am just out of the shower and go to fetch my robe from the bedroom. He is suddenly behind me and I sense his arousal. I quickly pull the robe around me, hiding my body. He spins me round and pushes me onto the bed. I try to roll over but he is on top of me. He parts the robe and begins to caress my breasts. My body cringes at his touch. I have always hated him touching me. His hand moves downwards. I am trapped between repulsion and fear of his guaranteed wrath if I pull away. My body decides for me, twisting to avoid him. He curses. His iron hands grab me and thrust me harshly onto the floor. The weight of my back lands on my arm and the pain shoots through me. My shoulder feels broken. He ignores my screams and storms out of the room. 'You fucking frigid bitch! You're not normal!' I remain where I am, trembling, a shattered doll.

Then one day, after spending over a third of my life with my husband, I met John. I had just started a new job and was busy trying to cope with the whirl of unfamiliar information. I remember being introduced to him and feeling struck by the kindness in his eyes and the gentleness of his manner. He wasn't conventionally good-looking – most women would pass him in the street without a second glance - but I saw a special beauty in him to which I felt drawn. The chemistry between us was tangible. When he looked at me, I felt like a goddess.

John invited me for coffee one morning before work. As we went to sit down, he took my coat. I felt foolish as a thrill ran through my body – such a simple, clichéd gesture but no man had ever done that for me before. As we chatted, I found that he was as giving and sensitive as his face suggested. He talked to me about the pain he felt over his own marriage breakdown and the poor treatment he had received from his wife. He was so open that, when it came my turn to share a glimpse of my married life, I found myself talking for the first time about the abuse.

When I explained my acceptance of the situation as my 'lot', John's compassion erupted. 'This is not your lot! There's no such thing – we create our own lives. You're young and beautiful. You shouldn't have to put up with anything that makes you unhappy!' At first I made excuses to justify Stuart's behaviour, saying that it was my fault because I let him get away with it and that the physical violence was fairly rare. John stated the universal truth that I guess I always knew. 'It should not happen even once.'

We talked more and more over the coming weeks. Seeing myself through John's eyes altered my outlook and gradually began to rebuild my sense of self-worth. John saw me as a proud and intelligent woman and I resented Stuart controlling me and treating me like a little girl. I didn't know whether I was in love with John, or he with me, but meeting him showed me everything that was missing from my relationship. I wanted respect.

For weeks I lay in bed, tormented, my body inches away from my husband but aching to be with someone else. Every time Stuart hurt me, my dissatisfaction grew. John had proved that there were men out there who saw women as precious creatures and would never dream of treating them as anything less. I wasn't condemned to this. I had a choice. It wouldn't be easy, but I knew I had to leave.

I kiss my mother- and father-in-law for the last time, my smile masking a torrent of emotions. I turn to Stuart and put my arms around him. 'See you tomorrow.' But we both know that I am returning to our home to move out, while he stays for the rest of the weekend with his parents. I collar my tears until I am on the train, then the sobs rise from my gut and pour out in passionate gasps. A woman sitting further down the carriage walks over and asks if I am all right. I wave her away and force myself to cry silently – I am well practised at this. The feeling is one of grief, as though I have just learnt of the death of a loved one. Everything I have known for 13 years is coming to a close and the unknown shadow world of the future is a frightening place.

Stuart crumbled when I left, unable to cope with the loss of control. A sense of guilt drove me to meet with him a few times and allow him the chance to talk. Each occasion brought an unbearable flood of mixed emotions. From tugging at my heartstrings with weeping apologies, promises that he would change and pleas for another chance, he would flick in an instant to a barrage of derisions and denial that he had done anything wrong. 'Fucking bitch, you're insane!' he would spit. 'You need help!' On the outside looking in, I saw his psychological games for what they were. I would simply look at him and say, 'This is why I'm never coming back.' He was cut by the ironic realisation that, after being dominated by him for so many years, I was actually the strong one.

Since leaving Stuart I have found strength in myself that I never imagined I had. I have surprised myself. The confidence, serenity and contentment I display to those around me feel genuine. Even the resentment I felt towards my husband has drained away, leaving only a deep sense of pity. I pray that one day he will make the effort to help himself.

John is no longer a part of my life. Fate deemed that he be one of those rare people who touch our lives at a time when we really need them and then fade away, all the more precious for the briefness of the encounter. But I don't give him credit for changing my life. He was the catalyst I needed, but I walked free on my own feet.

As I write, the divorce papers are on their way to my old home. I now rent a studio flat. It's comparatively tiny but I feel I have all the room to breathe I need. Naturally, I have bouts of sadness, but they always pass. I have come to see the highs and the lows as all part of the richness and diversity of the human experience. Though it may appear crushed, broken or just hard to find, hope is always within our grasp.

The first few steps are painful, as though the iron ring is still bound tightly, cutting into her flesh. But gradually the elephant's feet remember what it feels like to walk free. She breathes the sweet, free air. Before her, the plains extend to kiss the open sky. The winds caress her face bringing promise of a future as yet unexplored. With a heart graced with happiness, she heads for somewhere just past the horizon.

Advice and Contacts

Making a safety plan for you or a friend

You or your friend are probably doing lots of things already to help you and your children remain safe whether you are in an abusive relationship or have recently left one. The only person who can stop an abusive partner / ex partner's violence is themselves, so we have to make plans in order to keep ourselves and our children safe:

- Think about the things you already do – go to friends in an emergency etc.
- Make plans for an emergency, for example if your partner kicks off in the middle of the night.
- Is it safe to let your neighbours know about what's going on? Could you ask them to call the police if they hear screaming or shouting from your house?
- Keep with you some emergency telephone numbers including: support workers, gp, solicitor, local safe house, children's schools etc.
- If you have someone you trust (best for it not to be a mutual friend or family member) you could leave an emergency bag for yourself and your children, packing: I.d, passports, birth certificates, money, bank books, credit card details, proof of benefits & benefits information, documents about your home, spare keys to the house, car etc. medication, crime reference numbers from previous incidents of dv, injunctions, address book, photos, jewellery, a change of clothes for all of you, and your children's favourite possession – do not leave this bag in the house where the perpetrator may possibly find it, as this may put you at further risk.
- If appropriate teach your children how to make a 999 call to the police – do they know their name, address & telephone number.

- If the perpetrator is kicking off stay to areas of the house that you feel safer (usually not in the kitchen or bathroom).
- Remember mobile phones can be tracked – consider this if leaving an abusive relationship.
- Try and chat through your plans with a specialist domestic abuse worker if you are thinking of leaving an abusive relationship – as this is often the most dangerous time.

There is more information about this on the Women's Aid website: www.womensaid.org.uk

Frequently Asked Questions!

• *What is an IDVA?*

IDVA stands for Independent Domestic Violence Advisor. This means a domestic violence support worker who is employed independently of the Police and Courts. They work with survivors at the highest risk of harm from domestic violence & abuse.

IDVA's work for different agencies, a lot of which are in the voluntary sector: they will work with survivors to assess their level of risk, help them to make safety plans and reduce the risk to them and their children. Survivors who are at the highest risk will be discussed at the local multi agency risk assessment conference (see below). All agencies both statutory and voluntary will share information and make plans to improve safety and reduce risk.

IDVA's offer practical support to survivors by not only providing information but also going with them to relevant agencies such as: Solicitors, Police, Family or Criminal Courts, Housing or Social Services. If the survivor wishes to stay in their own home the IDVA can arrange for safety to be improved through new locks and alarms etc. Idva's will also support clients if they want to report to the Police, go through the Criminal Courts, or need to get Injunctions, Occupation Orders, or Residency Orders through the Civil Courts.

The work of the IDVA is short term and safety focused. Survivors can then be passed on to local domestic abuse outreach or resettlement services once the immediate risk has been reduced. The Knowle West Domestic Abuse Project provides both the IDVA and Outreach services in the area.

In Bristol the Knowle West Domestic Abuse Project, WISH for a Brighter Future (Hartcliffe & Withywood), Nextlink and Victim Support all have IDVA's working for them. (see useful contacts for more information).

- ***What is a MARAC?***

MARAC stands for Multi Agency Risk Assessment Conference: in Bristol this is led by the Police and includes members from Housing, Health, Education, Children & Young Peoples Services (Social Services), Probation Service and Voluntary Sector agencies such as specialist domestic abuse projects & drugs and alcohol agencies etc.

- ***What happens at a MARAC?***

There a two MARAC's a month in Bristol - one in the North and one in the South of the city; any agency can refer someone who is at high risk. Agencies check their records to see if they have worked with the family, and then share relevant information with the other agencies to help to safety plan and reduce the risk of significant harm to the survivor and their children. Bristol currently sees over 50 families a month through the MARAC process.

- ***Do I have to attend?***

The survivor does not attend the MARAC, but they can work with an IDVA who will be able to speak on their behalf, letting everyone know their thoughts, feelings, worries and concerns. The IDVA will also report back what actions will be taken by the agencies present.

- ***What is a Specialist Domestic Violence Court?***

An SDVC is a Specialist Domestic Violence Court: In Bristol this is held at the Magistrates court on a Tuesday & Thursday. All cases relating to domestic violence and abuse should be listed to be heard at the specialist courts by specially trained magistrates. IDVA's will be present at court all day to offer extra support through the whole court process to victims / witnesses.

- ***How can I protect myself if I don't want to go to the police?***

Survivors seek civil remedies as added protection, or as an alternative to going to the Police. First of all you visit a solicitor who specialises in family law / domestic violence, if the survivor's on benefits or a low income then you may be eligible for legal aid (which means you do not have to pay). The most common civil remedies used when someone is suffering domestic violence & abuse are injunctions: non molestation orders that the county court issue to the perpetrator to stay away from, not to contact, or get anyone else to contact the survivor. As well as occupation orders where the county court determine who should live in a property, whether it is privately owned or rented, and if one of the occupants is being violent and abusive to the other then the county court will probably make the decision that the survivor should occupy the home, and the perpetrator should leave. Another common order is a residency order that allows the county court to determine which parent the children should reside with. The breach of an injunction is now an arrestable offence.

- ***What if I want to stay in my own home?***

A Sanctuary Scheme provides free locks, alarms, safe rooms and other safety measures for survivor's homes. Sanctuary schemes are run by different agencies in different areas, some are run by the voluntary sector, others by housing providers and some by the police. In Bristol we can access the sanctuary scheme through the Bobby Van: the Bobby Van is a carpenter employed by the police to provide free advice, safety assessments and fit locks etc in survivor's homes. Then injunctions etc can be sought to help keep you safe (see question above).

- ***What's the Freedom Programme?***

The Freedom Programme is a 12 week support group for women. It is run as a rolling programme which means you can join at any point. The benefits are the same as long as you complete 12 weeks. The Freedom Programme is open to any woman who wishes to learn more about the reality of domestic abuse. The aims of the programme are:

- To help women to understand the beliefs held by abusive men and in so doing, recognise which of these beliefs they have shared.
- To show the effects of domestic abuse on children
- To help women to recognise potential future abusers.
- To help women to gain self esteem and the confidence to improve the quality of their lives.

- To introduce women to community resources such as specialist domestic abuse agencies: Knowle West Domestic Abuse Project, WISH, Nextlink & Victim Support, Police Domestic Abuse Investigation Teams and the Bristol Domestic Abuse Forums.

The Freedom Programme is run at various sites across the city, and indeed across the country. To find out about the programmes in Bristol phone: 0117 9142232. To find out about programmes in other areas of the country visit: www.freedomprogramme.co.uk

Knowle West Health Association
0117 9639569
Advocacy Project
Domestic Abuse Project
Community Kitchen Project
Over 50's club
Keep Fit
It's a Man Thing
Wow Group
Reminiscence Project
Creche
Foster Carers Support Group

Useful contacts

Bristol Area

Bristol Domestic Abuse Freephone Line (24 hr) – 0800 694 9999

Knowle West Domestic Abuse Project – 0117 9639569
(supporting women & men experiencing domestic abuse in the Knowle West and surrounding areas)
www.knowlewestdomesticabuse.co.uk

Wish – 0117 9038632
(supporting women & men experiencing domestic abuse in the Hartcliffe & Withywood areas)
www.wishforabrighterfuture.org.uk

Next Link – 0117 9250680
(refuge space, crisis & resettlement support for women across Bristol)
www.nextlinkhousing.co.uk

Victim Support Avonvale – 0845 456 6099
(support all victims of crime across Bristol & have specialist domestic abuse workers)
www.victimsupport.org.uk

Local Police – 0845 456 7000

Legal Advice Helpline (24 hr) – 0117 9045999

Nationwide

Women's Aid Freephone helpline (24 hr) - 0808 2000 247
(doesn't show up on the phone bill)
www.womensaid.org.uk

MALE Advice Line – 0845 064 6800
(for men experiencing domestic abuse)
www.mensadviceline.org.uk

Childline Freephone (24 hr) – 0800 1111
(for any child or young person needing to talk about anything)

Broken Rainbow – 0845 260 4460
(for Lesbian, Gay, Bisexual & Transgender people experiencing domestic abuse)
www.broken-rainbow.org.uk

Respect – 0845 122 8609
(for perpetrators of domestic abuse & organisations working with them)
www.respect.uk.net

RSPCA Pet Safe – 07715 540 182
(fostering service for animals)

Other Useful Websites

www.hiddenhurt.co.uk
(website where survivors share stories and information)

www.womankindbristol.org.uk
(women's counselling and helpline agency)

www.bdaf.org
(Bristol Domestic Abuse Forum's website)

www.thehideout.org.uk
(website for children & young people about DV)

The Clothesline Project (South Bristol)

The Clothesline Project is a visual display of t-shirts with graphic messages designed by women and children survivors of domestic and sexual violence. The T-shirts hang on a clothesline display to 'break the silence' and 'bear witness' to violence against women and children. The clothesline project seeks to help survivors with the healing process and to raise awareness of the issues.

For further information about the clothesline project email karen@knowlewesthealthassoc.org.uk or phone the Knowle West Domestic Abuse Project on 0117 9639569.